?

WORLD IN VIEW
SCOTLAND
Doreen Taylor

STECK-VAUGHN
L I B R A R Y
Austin, Texas

Library of Congress Cataloging-in-Publication Data

Taylor, Doreen, 1940–
   Scotland/Doreen Taylor.
     p. cm.—(World in view)
   Includes index.
   Summary: A general survey of Scotland, including its early
tribes, landscape, people, economics, and industries.
   ISBN 0-8114-2431-6
   1. Scotland—Juvenile literature. [1. Scotland.] I. Title.
II. Series.
DA762.T36 1991
941.1—dc20

                                     90-10028
                                        CIP
                                        AC

Cover: *Eilean Donan Castle, Loch Duich*
Title page: *Kilted pipers on parade*

Designed by Julian Holland Publishing Ltd
Picture research by Jennifer Johnson

Printed and bound in the United States
1 2 3 4 5 6 7 8 9 0 LB 95 94 93 92 91

Photographic credits:
Cover: Spectrum Colour Library, title page: Aviemore Photographic, 7 AA Picture Library, 8 J. Allan Cash, 9 Scottish Tourist Board, 10 Charles Tait, 11 M. Sinclair, 13 Christopher Mylne, 16 Charles Tait, 18 Mary Evans Picture Library, 22 Topham Picture Library, 28 AA Picture Library, 29 Scottish Tourist Board, 32 Hugh Martin and Partners, 33 Peter Dazeley Photography, 34 Aviemore Photographic, 37 AA Picture Library, 39 BP, 41, 42 AA Picture Library, 43 Scottish Development Agency, 45 Scottish Tourist Board, 46 Aviemore Photographic, 49 A Shell Photograph, 52 Scottish Tourist Board, 54 Paul Tomkins/Scottish Tourist Board, 56 Scottish Tourist Board, 57 AA Picture Library, 58 Hulton Picture Library, 59 Charles Tait, 60 AA Picture Library, 61, 62 Forestry Commission, 64 Scottish Tourist Board, 65 Christopher Mylne, 68 Scottish Tourist Board, 69 The Whithorn Trust, 70 The Scottish Tourist Board, 74 Topham Picture Library, 76 North of Scotland Hydro Electric Board, 77, 80 Charles Tait, 81 Paul Tomkins/Scottish Tourist Board, 82, 85, 87 Charles Tait, 88 Christopher Mylne, 91 AA Picture Library.

Contents

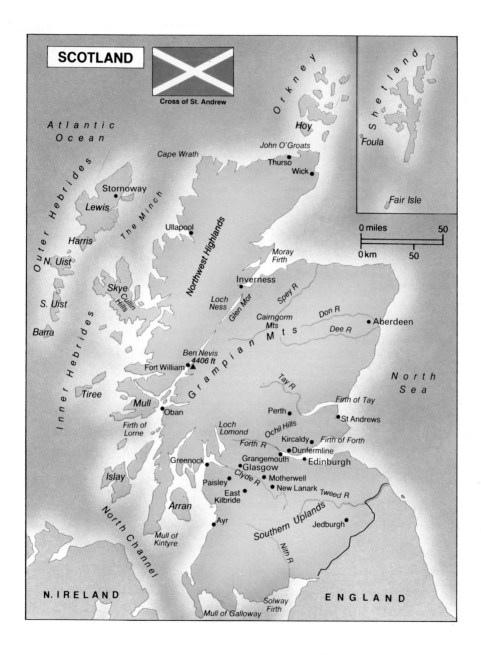

SCOTLAND

Cross of St. Andrew

Atlantic
Ocean

Orkney

Hoy

John O'Groats

Shetland

Foula

Cape Wrath

Thurso
Wick

Fair Isle

Outer Hebrides

Stornoway

Lewis

The Minch

Harris

N. Uist

Ullapool

Northwest Highlands

Moray
Firth

0 miles 50

0 km 50

Skye
Cullin
Hills

Inverness

Loch
Ness

Glen Mor

Spey R

S. Uist

Cairngorm
Mts

Don R

Dee R

Aberdeen

Barra

Inner Hebrides

Grampian Mts

North
Sea

Ben Nevis
4406 ft
Fort William

Tiree

Mull

Oban

Tay R

Firth of Tay

Perth

St Andrews

Firth of
Lorne

Loch
Lomond

Ochil Hills

Forth R

Kircaldy

Firth of Forth

Dunfermline

Greenock

Grangemouth

Edinburgh

Glasgow

Islay

Paisley

Clyde R

Motherwell

New Lanark

Tweed R

East
Kilbride

Arran

Ayr

Southern Uplands

Jedburgh

North Channel

Mull of
Kintyre

Nith R

N. IRELAND

ENGLAND

Solway
Firth

Mull of Galloway

1   Introduction

Scotland is the northern part of the island of Great Britain, which also includes the countries of England and Wales. On the west and north coasts is the Atlantic Ocean, and the North Sea bounds the east. To the south Scotland borders England.

Scotland has more than one-third of Britain's land area, but only around one-tenth of the total population of the island. It is one of the least-crowded countries in the western part of Europe, with around 170 people per square mile. By comparison, England has 920 people per square mile.

A small country
Scotland is small. The greatest distance from north to south is only 275 miles while the greatest width is 154 miles. The country is narrowest in the Central Lowlands between the estuaries of the Forth and Clyde rivers. This narrow section of the country is known as the Central Belt. Few parts of Scotland are farther than 40 miles from the sea or an estuary.

Although Scotland is not a large country, it has great variety. It has the highest mountains in Britain and the colors on the green hillsides change with the seasons, from the purple of summer heather to brown and orange when the bracken dies in autumn. The landscape includes lowlands, steep river courses, fast-flowing hill burns (streams), and some 609 square miles of freshwater lochs (lakes). There are haughs (low-lying riverside meadows) and marshy riverside

groves called carseland.

The coastline is more than 2,000 miles long and varies from stretches of wide, open beaches to deeply indented, rocky shores, where the sea cuts into the land to form headlands and inlets. Nearly 800 islands, some of several hundred square miles, others just large rocks, lie off the Scottish coast, mostly to the west and north.

Links with Europe

Once the Picts and Scots had stopped fighting each other, their attention turned toward the threat of invasion by the English. France offered

The Corrieshallow Gorge falls steeply through the Braemore Forest, creating dramatic waterfalls. There are numerous waterfalls in Scotland as a result of the mountainous terrain and good rainfall.

Staffa's lava pillars are at their most magnificent in Fingal's Cave, celebrated in Mendelssohn's overture of the same name. Legend has it that the cave was once linked to a similar feature, the Giant's Causeway in Northern Ireland, on the other side of the Irish Sea.

geographical areas that, in turn, can be subdivided. The first of these three areas lies to the northwest of a line from Helenburgh in the west to Stonehaven in the east. This area is known as the Highlands.

The rift valley, which lies between the south of this line and another fault line running from Girvan in the west to Dunbar on the east coast, forms the Central Lowlands. To call this area "Lowlands" is rather misleading because the region also includes a number of hill ranges, as well as rich, rolling farmland.

The country to the south of the Girvan/Dunbar fault line is the Southern Uplands, with seven major hill ranges. This is largely high hill country, with green, rounded tops rather than the jagged peaks of the north. The area's highest peak, the Merrick, in the Galloway Hills, reaches only 2,764 feet, although there are some other high peaks. These peaks such as Criffell, which overlooks the Solway Firth, are made up of the hard, coarse-grained rock called granite.

The land and water boundaries with England lie along the Cheviot Hills, the Solway Firth, and the lower reaches of the Liddel and Tweed rivers.

The Highlands

The Highlands are made up largely of very hard types of rock that have resisted ice, wind, and water with greater success than anywhere else in Scotland. The Highland landscape was scoured to its present form by the Ice Age more than 15,000 years ago. Many rivers flow through

The steep face of Ben Nevis looms over the surrounding Highlands and the town of Fort William. At 4,406 feet high, Ben Nevis is the highest mountain in Britain. Highland cattle graze on the bleak pastures.

broad valleys, or glens, scraped out by the ice, and the smaller rivers and mountain burns fall swiftly through steep hanging valleys. These are valleys that have been cut across by a glacier so that they now enter, high up on the sides, a deeper steep-walled main valley that has been eroded by ice.

The islands to the west have great variety. On Skye and Mull, lava, deposited when these islands were volcanic, long before the Ice Age, has formed flat tables of rock. On the island of Staffa, lava has cooled and cracked to form great six-sided pillars of rock. The oldest rock in Scotland is to be found on Lewis. On the mainland the highest mountains are the Grampian Highlands in the east, and the great range of the Cairngorms. The northwest

In the far northeast of Scotland is the lowland plain of Caithness. The area is thinly populated, but the small town of Wick, once Europe's biggest herring port, serves as a center for a large area.

Highland mass tilts toward the west coast and the rivers on this side are fast-flowing. The rivers that flow to the North Sea in the east, such as the famous salmon river, the Spey, and the Don and Dee rivers vary from rushing shallows to their deeper, slower reaches.

The Highlands also have their lowland areas that in many ways are more like the Central Lowlands than the northwest. They include the rich farming land around Aberdeen, the eastern coastal strip, the peninsula of Buchan, and the land on either side of the Moray Firth.

The Central Lowlands

This region is some 120 miles from southeast to northwest and 50 miles wide. It contains well over half of Scotland's population.

The coast of southwest Scotland is made up of numerous inlets or lochs, surrounded by gently sloping hills. Small fishing villages are found all along the coast.

This rift valley came into being when the ground subsided between the two fault lines to the north and south. The eastern part contains Scotland's longest river, the Tay, which is 118 miles long and passes the "Fair City" of Perth. Scotland's fourth-largest city, Dundee, is at its estuary. To the west is the great Clyde River which flows through lovely countryside and the city of Glasgow.

Although this region is largely lowland, it contains several hill ranges such as the Lammermuirs, Moorfoots, and Pentland Hills to the south of the area. On either side of the Tay River lie the Sidlaw and Ochil Hills, and to the west are the Campsie Fells and the Kilpatrick Hills.

The Southern Uplands
In the south, the hills are not as high as the Highland mountains, and the rivers are less steep than the west-flowing rivers of the northern Highlands. The Tweed River basin has the Lammermuirs and Moorfoot Hills to the north, as it flows from headwaters in Tweeddale, not far from the source of the Clyde River, to its wide mouth at Berwick-upon-Tweed, on the English side of the border. Its many tributaries divide the Borderland, which forms the eastern area of the Southern Uplands. This is a beautiful, fertile land of rolling green hills, rich in legend and story that provided material for the writer, Sir Walter Scott.

The western area is the region of Dumfries and Galloway and in the east it has many similarities with the Borders, in both geography and history. Farther west, in Galloway, the high rolling

Sir Walter Scott
The novelist Sir Walter Scott (1771–1832) immortalized the Borders when he published *The Minstrelsy of the Scottish Borders.* A lawyer by profession, he became Sheriff of Selkirkshire in 1799, and his great house at Abbotsford is still occupied by his descendants. Scott, it is claimed, invented the novel with volumes such as *Redgauntlet, The Heart of Midlothian,* and *The Bride of Lammermoor.*

The warm Gulf Stream, which washes the coast of northwest Scotland, produces a milder climate than in other parts of Scotland. It is possible to grow a wide variety of plants, and several large houses such as Inverewe open their gardens to the public.

uplands and bare granite rocks of the Galloway Hills tilt south toward the Solway Firth to become a coastal strip. The two peninsulas, the Rhinns and the Machars of Wigtownshire in the far southwest, are the remains of a submerged coast. The Rhinns coast, in particular, is grassland above

rocky cliffs, where the sea cuts into the land in deep inlets, known locally as *slunks*. The area's only sea loch is Loch Ryan, which faces north on the west coast, and farther inland is the long, narrow shape of Loch Ken, a wintering ground for geese.

Climate

The Scottish weather can be cold and very windy, sometimes harsh on the higher ground and, especially in the west, very wet. At the same time, compared to Canadian and Scandinavian cities of the same latitude, Scotland has a remarkably temperate climate.

The seas on the west coast are warmed by the Gulf Stream that travels across the South Atlantic from the Gulf of Mexico. The west coast therefore experiences mild temperatures but the prevailing westerly winds also mean the largest amount of rainfall in Scotland. In comparison, the east of the country is influenced by its nearness to the cold of northern Europe and is much cooler. The climate of the high central mountains is less influenced by the sea, and the mountains' quick weather changes, bringing sudden hill mists and strong chilling winds or heavy snow, are dangerous and usually the cause of Scotland's mountain accidents.

The greatest characteristic of Scottish weather is its variety, and many days include rain, sun, and gusting winds. Snow in the northwest Highlands can be replaced by brief spells in the summer when the temperatures can reach 80°F.

2 Rebellions, Religion, and Recovery

People first came to Scotland over 6,000 years ago, as the last remains of the Ice Age crept slowly north. Little is known about these early tribes but it is generally believed that they came from Ireland and were hunters and fishermen.

Recorded history

Recorded history began around A.D. 90, when an army led by the Roman general Agricola managed to push as far north as the Tay River. The result was to unify the restless tribes living in the region who had been fighting each other. United, they fought so fiercely they drove the Romans south once more. The Romans, who called them Picts, which meant "the painted people," found them fierce enemies. In 118, the Roman Ninth Legion marched north to subdue "the savages," and simply disappeared. The Romans never conquered these northern tribes. Instead, they built two great walls against them.

The name Scotland comes from the Scoti, a tribe who settled in Scotland from Ireland during the fifth century. Over the next 200 years they fought, but also intermarried with, the Picts. By 844, Kenneth MacAlpin became King of Picts and Scots. In 1025, the Scots took over Lothian in the southeast, and Kenneth MacAlpin's descendant, Malcolm II, ruled over an area with boundaries similar to those of Scotland today.

15

Hadrian's Wall was the first wall built by the Romans to keep the northern tribes at bay. It was built of stone and was completed in 127. It was so strong that today its huge ramparts still march across the north of England, just south of the present border. In 143, the Romans built a second barrier made of turf and earth.

Links with Europe

Once the Picts and Scots had stopped fighting each other, their attention turned toward the threat of invasion by the English. France offered support and the links between France and Scotland strengthened with a treaty called the "Auld Alliance" (Old Alliance) and with intermarriage between the two royal families. The ties with France and the rest of Europe were to influence Scottish trade, architecture, and culture.

At home, the troubled border between Scotland and England moved back and forth according to which country was winning in a series of border wars. Warrior kings of England such as Edward I, "the Hammer of the Scots," claimed sovereignty over Scotland, and both sides raided across the border.

An independent nation

In 1314, Robert the Bruce, who was King of Scotland, defeated the English at Bannockburn. This was one of Scotland's greatest battles. Bruce was eager that other nations should acknowledge his kingship and put pressure on the English to confirm Scotland's independence. The Scots sent the Declaration or Arbroath to the Pope in Rome which confirmed their loyalty to Bruce as king, and included the words: "While there exist a hundred of us, we will never submit to England. We fight not for glory, wealth, or honour, but for that liberty without which no virtuous man shall survive." In 1328, Edward III of England confirmed Scotland's full independence. Bruce was succeeded in 1371 by the Stewart or Stuart monarchs. From that date until the Union of the Crowns in 1603, when James VI of Scotland also became James I of England, Scotland was full of internal strife.

Mary, Queen of Scots

Mary, Queen of Scots, Scotland's best-known and most tragic queen, was only a week old when

Mary Queen of Scots was executed in 1587 by Elizabeth I of England, who saw the Scottish queen as a rival for her own throne.

she became queen in 1542. She was brought up in France, married the French king and, on his death in 1560, returned to Scotland to take up her throne.

Mary's reign was stormy. The creation of the Church of Scotland under John Knox meant that Scotland was rapidly becoming a Protestant country. Mary's second husband, Henry Darnly, was found murdered and she quickly married James Hepburn, Earl of Bothwell, who was Protestant. In 1567, Mary was forced by Bothwell to give up her throne in favor of her son. She fled to England for protection only to be executed after years of imprisonment on the orders of her cousin, Queen Elizabeth I of England.

The united kingdom

When Queen Elizabeth died in 1603, she left no children. James VI of Scotland, Mary's son, inherited the throne and became James I of both

The Highland Clans

From as early as the sixth century there was a clan system in Scotland. In the north the clans were like big families, each member of a clan owing loyalty to a single chief such as Campbell, Cameron, MacDonald, and MacGregor. Later, as surnames became more common, clan members took on the name of their chief and each clan began to develop its own tartan (plaid woolen) cloth. For each clan there was a special tartan. The clan system was never strong in the south though many families ruled large areas of land. There, people spoke Lowland Scots, a variation of English. The Highland clans, who spoke only Gaelic, were to remain strong until the eighteenth century.

When King William came to the throne in England, he was determined that the Highland clans were to become loyal to him as they had been to the Stuart kings before him. He made them swear an oath to himself that led to one of the most famous killings in Scottish history.

In 1692, MacDonald of Glencoe arrived too late to swear his oath. With this as an excuse, the royal agents in Scotland sent members of Clan Campbell, who were loyal to the new king, to visit the MacDonalds. Although the two clans had long been enemies, the Campbells said they came in friendship. In the middle of the night they obeyed their secret orders and killed every male MacDonald between the ages of seven and 70, an act that has never been forgotten.

Scotland and England, and moved the court to London.

Now that England and Scotland shared the same king, the next step was the Union of Parliaments. Against a wave of disapproval, this was pushed through the Scottish Parliament by a group of nobles, and was accepted gaining Scotland the right of free trade across the border as well as trading access to the English colonies.

The Stuart kings remained on the throne for three generations until James II, who took up the Catholic faith of his great-grandmother, was deposed in 1689 in favor of the Protestant Dutch Prince, William of Orange.

Rebellions

Even though William was on the throne, the Stuarts were not finished. The first attempt to restore a Stuart monarch was made in 1715 by James II's son, James Stuart, who managed to unite many Highland clans but did not succeed in the campaign that became known as The Fifteen. In 1745, James' son Prince Charles Edward Stuart, known as "Bonnie Prince Charlie," looked at first as though he might succeed.

He landed from France, gathered the clans together and his Highland army defeated the English at Prestonpans. However, he was finally defeated in 1746, at the battle of Culloden near Inverness.

The Age of Enlightenment

With the new prosperity brought by free trade across the border into England and its colonies under the Union of Parliaments, Scotland, and

"Bonnie Prince Charlie" rides through the streets of Edinburgh with his Highland supporters before his defeat at the battle of Culloden. After the battle he was helped by Flora MacDonald to reach the Isle of Skye. After months as a fugitive he was picked up by a ship and sailed for France, never to return to Scotland. The Skye Boat Song *commemorates his flight.*

The Highland Clearances
The Union of Parliaments saw the start of the great Scottish migration throughout the world. Sometimes people left to seek a better life in the newer countries of America and Australia. Others had no choice and left during the Highland Clearances of the late eighteenth and early nineteenth century when the Highland landowners decided that sheep would be more profitable than people. They evicted their tenants from their crofts (small farms), and shipped them to America.

particularly Edinburgh, moved into what is known as the Age of Enlightenment. During this period Scotland produced many philosophers, economists, writers, painters, politicians, and inventors. The Age of Enlightenment was at its height in the late eighteenth century and lasted until the middle of the nineteenth century.

The Industrial Revolution

This period was also the time of the Scottish Industrial Revolution. Glasgow was already a center of the tobacco trade and then, in 1760, the Carron Ironworks was opened at Falkirk, with

Ramsay MacDonald (1866–1937), the Scot who became Britain's first Labour Prime Minister, making a speech about industrial disputes.

the main purpose of making weapons. Many new industries followed, such as heavy engineering, shipbuilding, mining, glass, pottery, and china-making, carpet-making, jute and other forms of weaving, distilling, and brewing.

These new industries called for new workers, who flocked into the cities from rural Scotland and across the sea from Ireland to the whole of the Central Belt, and particularly to Glasgow. The new industries also brought radical ideas of freedom and equality, inspired by the French Revolution. At that time, only 4,500 Scots had the right to vote. Complaints over the injustice of the Scottish voting system led to riots, arrests, deportation, and even hanging. In 1832, the Reform Bill extended the right to vote to 65,000 Scots, a step toward votes for all adults.

Revolution in labor

The start of the Scottish Labour Party in 1888 marked the beginning of the British Labour Party, and Scotland voted in Britain's first Labour Member of Parliament (MP), Keir Hardie.

In World War I, Scots made up 15 percent of the British Army, and 20 percent of all Britons killed were Scots. The shipyard workers, who were producing more tanks, warships, and weapons than anywhere else in Britain during the war, fought for better working conditions. The strikes and industrial disputes between 1915 and 1919 led to the area being named "Red Clydeside." When the men went on strike for shorter working hours in 1919 they were put down with military force by the order of the Secretary of State for Scotland.

Industry declines

After World War I, Scottish industry had a few more years of hard work and wealth before the large-scale industries declined.

Not until World War II, when every factory was once more in full production, did Scottish industry recover, but the war also brought danger and the problem of shortages. In 1941, the shipyard town of Clydebank was almost completely destroyed in two nights of heavy bombing that killed 1,000 people.

Although industry declined again after the war, in the late 1960s oil was discovered in the North Sea. The profit from this new industry helped the British economy in general rather than Scotland. This fact has given rise to a new wave of Scottish nationalism, and in 1974, the Scottish National Party used the slogan "It's Scotland's Oil" to get eleven Scottish National Party members elected to Parliament. This election also strengthened the movement for a separate Scottish Assembly.

3   Scotland Today

After the Act of Union, Scotland was at first governed from London but, in 1885, a Secretary for Scotland was appointed to head the Scottish Office, which now has its headquarters in Edinburgh and an office in London. By 1926, the post was upgraded to Secretary of State with a seat in the British cabinet. When Scottish business is debated in the House of Commons, the Secretary of State is responsible for the government's arguments.

Since a Conservative government took over in 1979, Scotland has continued to vote Labour in the majority of its 72 parliamentary seats. In the 1987 general election, Scotland returned 50 Labour MPs, 10 Conservatives, and 12 MPs of other parties.

Scottish people look on themselves first and foremost as Scots, then British, but never English. Nearly 300 years after the Union, some Scots still believe that Scotland should be independent and have its own parliament to control its domestic affairs. Nevertheless, when the Scots held a special vote in 1979, to decide whether they should have their own parliament, the result was equally divided between "yes" and "no," and one-third did not vote at all.

Local government

The Act of Union guaranteed Scotland's separate legal system and the national church, and today Scotland also retains separate systems of education and organizations that cover aspects of life from industry and economic development to sports, tourism, and conservation.

Since 1975, Scotland has been divided into nine regions, each of which has its own Regional Council. The regions are the Borders, Central, Dumfries and Galloway, Fife, Grampian, Highland, Lothian, Strathclyde, and Tayside.

Each Regional Council is responsible for taking care of certain aspects of life in its area, such as schools, police, and industrial development. The Regional Councils are all divided into smaller districts, 53 in all, which deal with other more local matters, for example, local planning, tourism, parks, and museums.

Three Island Councils combine the functions of both region and district for the western and northern islands. The three councils are Western Isles, Orkney, and Shetland.

Scottish law
Scottish law is different from English law, and also from law in countries such as the United States and the British Commonwealth, who based their law systems on England's. Scottish law is based on Roman law, and has more in common with European codes, which may be due to Scotland's early ties with the Continent.

The main difference is that Scottish juries have a choice of three verdicts: "guilty," "not guilty," or "not proven." "Not proven" means that the jury has not been able to decide on guilt or innocence, and gives the accused the benefit of the doubt.

There are two types of Scottish lawyer. Solicitors deal with a wide range of affairs, from buying and selling houses to wills and divorces.

They can appear personally in the lower courts, but advocates do most of the court work.

Children and young people under 16 who are accused of an offense in Scotland usually do not have to go to an adult court. They are dealt with at Children's Hearings by a special panel of people who decide what is best for the child. The panel has a lawyer known as the Children's Reporter to help them

Education

By law children in Scotland must go to school between the ages of five and 16. Many attend a nursery school or play group before they are five. Around half of all school pupils continue their education after they are 16.

Most schools are coed and free, and are provided by local education authorities in each region. Only around 3.5 percent of Scottish pupils attend schools that charge tuition.

The first school for most Scottish children is their local primary school. These schools vary in size from several hundred pupils to just a few pupils with only one teacher in country areas. School ends at around 3:30 p.m. each day and often earlier for younger pupils. Because Scotland is so far north, in winter it is dark when children leave for school in the morning and dark again by the time they return home.

Most pupils go to primary school for seven years and then move on to secondary school when they are around 12 years old.

At the end of their second year at secondary school the pupils choose which subjects they will follow in later years. The general aim in Scotland

Some pupils, like these children from Leverburgh on South Harris, go to school each day by local motorboat. In the remoter parts of the Highlands and the Islands, it is not always possible to provide secondary education. Some pupils have to go away to school during the week and return home on Friday.

is to keep as wide and well-balanced a range as possible. The pupils take the Scottish Certificate of Education which can be taken at both ordinary and higher grades. Many of those who have done higher grades go on to a university.

Scotland has eight universities, four old, four new, with a total of around 47,000 students. For a long time, the Scottish tradition was for students, if possible, to live at home and attend the university in their own city. This has now changed and many students live away from home, while students from other parts of Britain and overseas also attend Scottish universities.

Students can also study for degrees at 16 colleges of higher education, and there are around 50 further education colleges specializing in many career-based subjects.

Religion

The national church is the Church of Scotland, a Presbyterian church. Under the Presbyterian system a congregation elects its own minister, either a man or woman. Each year the church elects a Moderator as head of the church. The Moderator presides over the General Assembly.

In its early days the church banned music, and its buildings were very plain. Later, it decided to bring in popular melodies to accompany the church's psalms. Many of these tunes, such as "Crimond," which accompanies the 23d psalm, are today sung all over the world.

The number of church members is just under 900,000 (1987) but many more Scots claim "a Christian way of life."

Iona is still Scotland's Holy Island and many people visit its abbey, which has been lovingly restored this century by a Christian group called the Iona Community.

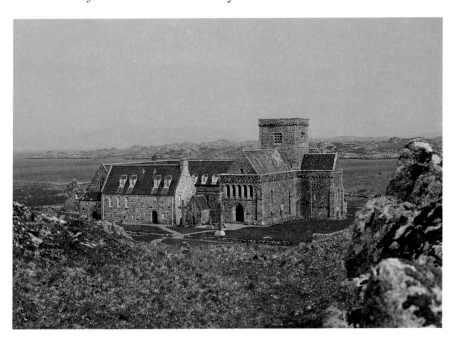

The Roman Catholic Church has some 800,000 members, making it the second largest church in Scotland. Remoter parts of Scotland, particularly some of the Western Isles, have always retained their Roman Catholic faith. Other Catholics may be descendants of Irish people who came to work in Scotland during the Industrial Revolution.

The other main protestant religion is the Scottish Episcopal Church, with a membership of around 40,000, and there is also a small Jewish community, with congregations in the four main cities. Small communities of Muslims, Hindus, Sikhs, and Buddhists live in Scotland too, but they make up a tiny segment of the population.

Health and welfare services

Since 1948, Scotland has had a National Health Service. Patients do not have to pay for doctors or hospital stays, but there are charges for some services such as dental and eye examinations, and for drug prescriptions. Children, elderly people, and pregnant women do not have to pay. Most babies are born in a hospital, although today some parents prefer to give birth at home. In the rural areas, the big general hospital may be a long way away, and it is sometimes difficult for relatives to visit.

Welfare Services cover unemployment, sickness, and other difficulties. Social welfare services also assist people with handicaps and children in need or in danger. A great deal of work is also done by volunteer groups, such as finding homes or providing services such as "Meals on Wheels," which brings meals to people who are housebound or unable to cook for themselves.

4 The Scottish People

The population of Scotland is just over five million, with 3.5 million living in the Central Lowlands, which consists of the capital, Edinburgh, Scotland's biggest city, Glasgow, and the area around Aberdeen. The other 1.5 million live in the sparsely populated Highlands and Islands to the northwest and the Borders and Galloway in the south.

Some 20 million people in different countries claim Scottish descent, four times more than live in Scotland itself. These people are very proud of their links with Scotland and many enjoy putting on their kilts on special occasions. Some play in Scottish bagpipe bands that have formed in many countries, and practice Scottish dancing. In recent years, the winner of the World Piping Championships at the Duke of Atholl's Castle at Blair Atholl has sometimes come from outside Scotland.

Scottish talents
Among the world's inventors, engineers, writers, political thinkers, and economists there have been many Scots. *The Study of British Genius* by the English scientist, Havelock Ellis, showed that although it formed only 10 percent of the British population, Scotland had produced more than 15 percent of its geniuses.

The father of modern economics, Adam Smith, was a Scot. Other famous Scots include the physicist James Clerk Maxwell, Sir James Young Simpson who discovered anaesthetics, and

Scottish architects still have an eye for elegance, as is shown by this extension to a classical nineteenth-century building in Glasgow. The new style was developed to reflect Glasgow's earlier important connections with Art Nouveau architecture and design at the beginning of this century.

Alexander Fleming who saved innumerable lives when he discovered penicillin. There was the philosopher David Hume, and a whole list of painters including David Wilkie and Henry Raeburn in the eighteenth century, and Anne Redpath and John Bellany in the twentieth. Scotland has also produced some very famous writers, from the poet Robert Burns to the author of *Treasure Island*, Robert Louis Stevenson. Architecture, too, has been much influenced by Scottish talent. Buildings and decoration by the great architects Robert and James Adam beautify all parts of Britain. Then there are the Scots who, having left the country of their birth, came to fame in various fields, from Alexander Graham Bell, who invented the telephone, to the industrialist Andrew Carnegie, who gave much of his wealth to libraries, education, and research.

Sports

Scotland has a long tradition of sports and while many of the games are played worldwide, Scots also have one or two distinctly their own.

A popular belief is that golf began in Scotland, although some people say it started in Holland and was brought to Scotland by seamen around 1450. Either way, the famous Old Course at St. Andrews is nicknamed "the home of golf" and there are more than 400 golf courses in Scotland.

Some people claim that soccer is the true "religion" of Scotland, and Scotland has its own national team to compete in European and world competitions. Rugby is also popular, particularly in the Borders of Scotland. To be a famous rugby player is the ambition of many small boys in the Borders and, in 1984, Border teams provided two-

St. Andrew's is the home of the world's most famous golf course, The Royal and Ancient Golf Club, founded in 1754.

Curling is now usually played on an ice rink, and has spread to Canada and Scandinavia.

thirds of the Scottish side that won the Grand Slam, the annual competition between Scotland, England, Ireland, Wales, and France.

Curling is thought to have started when, during the winter frosts, farmers were unable to work outside. To amuse themselves they began to slide smooth stones along the ice, to see which one would finish closest to a target.

Shinty was played in the Highlands before the seventeenth century, and is rare outside Scotland. It is a sort of hockey but the difference is in the free use of the stick or *caman*. It is a fast, fierce game that, to the onlooker, seems to have no rules. Today, there are some 40 clubs, mostly in the towns and villages of the Highlands, although most cities also have a team. Shinty's closest relative is the Irish game of hurling.

Language

Scotland originally had two languages, Gaelic and Scots. Scots is a language similar to English spoken in Lowland Scotland, including the northeast. It was once a separate, written language, but after the crowns united in 1603, and the court moved south, educated Scottish people began to write in English. Scots then became a spoken language only and gradually less widely used.

Today, almost all Scots have some trace of a

Some Scots Words

ain	one
ashet	large plate of meat
bairn or we'an	child
breeks	breeches or trousers
carnaptious	irritable, quarrelsome
cloot	cloth
clootie dumpling	pudding boiled in cloth
dowfie	sad, depressed
drouthy	thirsty
footery	fiddly, intricate
glaikit	stupid
hame	home
ken	know
kirk	church
kist	wooden chest (box)
lum	chimney
moggie	cat
redd up	clean up, put in order
runkled	wrinkled
scunnered	to be sick of, fed up with
to thole	to put up with
wee	little, small
yon or thot	that (yon hill)
yon brae	that hill

Scottish accent. They also use Scots words and phrases, which are often very expressive. To given one example, for the English verb "to limp," the Scots say "to hirple," which sounds much more like the action it describes than the English version.

Even within Scotland, different areas have their own dialects that can vary greatly. The Highland town of Inverness, however, is said to speak the purest English in Britain. Invernesians tend to use correct English grammar when speaking, something other English speakers rarely do, but their accent is pure Scots.

The northwest Highlands and Islands are the home of Scotland's second language, Gaelic, an ancient tongue which is now spoken by less than 100,000 people. Two generations ago almost everyone in the Western Highlands and the Islands would have spoken Gaelic. Then came a time when children were discouraged from using their native tongue, in the belief that English would be of more use in later life, although Gaelic was still spoken at home.

The early 1980s saw a revival of interest in Gaelic, and a new emphasis has been put on the teaching and speaking of Gaelic at home and at work. Road signs are in both Gaelic and English in the Outer Hebrides and it is taught, with English, in many schools. The two Scottish independent television (ITV) companies, Scottish Television and Grampian, as well as BBC Scotland, all broadcast programs in Gaelic. Stornaway, on the island of Lewis, is the main base of BBC Scotland's Gaelic radio service.

5 Living and Working

The area where the greatest number of people live in Scotland stretches across the Central Belt of Scotland and takes in most of the Lothian Region, the south of Fife and Central Regions, and the urban areas of Scotland's largest region, Strathclyde. The area around Dundee and the northeastern city of Aberdeen, now Scotland's oil capital, are the next most-populated areas. The rural areas of the north and south are mostly sparsely populated.

Almost one-third of all Scots live in the four main cities. Glasgow has a population of 725,000, Edinburgh 438,000, Dundee 176,000 and Aberdeen 216,000. Aberdeen is the only city where the population has grown over the past 20 years, largely due to the discovery of North Sea oil.

Some employers like Robert Owen, who built a "model village" at New Lanark, believed in good homes, schools, and health education for their workers. Today, New Lanark has been restored and is a popular place to live in or visit.

The rises and falls in industry

For centuries, people had known that the Central Belt was rich in mineral deposits, and lead was mined there as early as the thirteenth century. Coal, too, was plentiful in the Forth Valley, Fife, and Lanarkshire and had been mined beginning in the fifteenth and sixteenth centuries.

Until the Industrial Revolution, despite these early industries, most trades were locally-based. Weavers and other handworkers worked in their own homes, and often depended on natural resources that were close at hand. In the early eighteenth century, Glasgow and the Clyde was a small trading center. The region's wealth was based largely on the tobacco trade and its dealings with the American colonies. During the American Revolution in the 1770s, the tobacco trade suffered badly and by the end of the century it had disappeared altogether. This collapse was also helped by the Industrial Revolution, which enabled people to leave the dying tobacco trade to work in new industries.

The new industries that were created also drew people from all over Scotland to come and live and work in the Central Belt, particularly

A Nation of Engineers

The late eighteenth and early nineteenth century produced some very fine engineers. Scottish engineers designed canals and built railroads and bridges to link the cities and remoter areas. The Scottish marine engineer became a familiar figure on ships all over the world, and enterprising young Scots took their talents and skills throughout the world.

British Petroleum's large petrochemical production complex at Grangemouth, which makes almost half of British Petroleum's ethylene, is linked by pipeline to other polyethylene producers such as the Shell-Esso plant at Mossorran in Fife.

Glasgow. The city's population grew from 17,000 in 1740 to 400,000 in 1870. By the mid–twentieth century, Glasgow had topped a million.

The flourishing industries of the nineteenth century made Scotland one of the most prosperous parts of Britain, but as other countries began to develop their own industries, such as iron and steel, their need for Scottish goods decreased and Scotland sold fewer of its traditional manufactured goods. In the 1920s and 1930s, almost one in three workers had no job, and life, particularly in Glasgow and the heavy industrial areas, became very hard.

World War II (1939–45) brought an industrial revival that lasted for nearly two decades, and the need to build houses and reequip was strong.

Then competition from Japan and other countries led to another decline in the traditional heavy industries of Scotland.

Change was on its way. New lighter industries, such as electronics, began to move in, and Scottish people began to learn new skills. These new industries began to make a contribution in providing jobs. However, with the economic decline throughout Britain unemployment increased threefold after 1979. In Scotland, it led to the closing of many traditional factories,

---

Where Scots Work Today

Manufacturing
The main manufacturing industries today are:
Chemicals
Minerals and mineral products
Food, drink, and tobacco
Paper, printing, and publishing
Mechanical manufacturing industries
Manufacture of metal goods
Textiles, clothing
Transportation equipment
Construction and building
Electricity, gas, and coal

Service industries
Oil and oil-related industries
Distribution and retailing — shops, etc.
Repairs and maintenance
Tourism, hotels, and catering
Banking, finance, insurance
Transportation and communications
Public Services (e.g., local government)
Medical and health services
Education

Although the Clyde's docks and wharves are no longer busy with shipping, a large Exhibition and Conference Center in Glasgow is bringing new service industries into the area.

shipyards, and coal mines, and many Scots lost their jobs. Today, unemployment is still higher in Scotland than the British average, and in some areas a quarter of the workers are out of a job. The average unemployment in 1988 was around 13 percent.

Gradually, the new light industries and the service industries are beginning to offer more jobs and the unemployment figure at last appears to be declining. In 1988, around two million people worked in paid jobs, almost half of them women. In addition, around one-tenth of working Scots are now self-employed, working in their own businesses or professions.

6 Scotland's Strengths

Scotland's move away from heavy industry has meant that the country has had to look to other areas for economic strength. This chapter looks at some of the success stories in Scotland's recent past.

New towns

After World War II, Glasgow and some other towns in west central Scotland became too overpopulated to be comfortable places to live or work in, which led to a housing shortage.

This area was open countryside when East Kilbride, the first new town, was started in 1947. It is now the biggest of the new towns, and the surrounding parks are well established.

The Clyde River flows through the center of Glasgow. At one time, the great river was lined with shipyards, wharves, and ships from all over

One of the Central Belt's new factories is built into an attractively landscaped industrial zone. The area where many of these factories are found has earned the nickname "Silicon Glen," after Silicon Valley in California.

to attract new industry to provide work for the people who moved there. The new towns that were built are East Kilbride (1947), Glenrothes (1948), Cumbernauld (1955), Livingstone (1962), and Irvine (1966).

The total number of people who live in the five new towns is just over a quarter of a million, and 91,000 people now have jobs there.

Electronics

Next to oil, the fastest-growing and most successful industry in recent years in Scotland has been the production of electronic equipment. This high-technology industry has quadrupled in size over the last 20 years. Many of these "high-tech" factories are concentrated in the Central Belt, although the industry has also spread out as

43

far as Dundee, Greenock and the Borders. Small factories are also moving into the Highlands.

The Borders, which have long been famous for high quality knitwear and tweed (largely in Hawick and Galashiels) have adapted particularly well to electronics. The new companies have found that the skilled fingers of men and women who were used to using intricate knitting and weaving machines could easily tackle printed circuits and delicate wiring systems.

Tourism

Scotland is one of the most beautiful countries in Europe and a popular place with people touring Europe. Queen Victoria's enthusiasm and love for the country was a great help to Scotland's early tourist industry. Soon people from all over the world were coming to visit this country with its Highlands and lochs, glens and castles. Queen Victoria and her husband, Prince Albert, turned their royal Castle of Balmoral into a "real" Scottish home, just as they imagined it had been when the old Scottish clan chiefs inhabited it. Even the carpets were patterned in the special Balmoral tartan that is only worn by the British royal family, and the royal household was wakened each day by a piper playing outside the castle. Today, Deeside, where Balmoral stands, is known as Royal Deeside.

Tourism has become one of the most important industries in Scotland and brings about $2.4 billion into the country annually. One important aspect of tourism is that hotels and resorts are often set in country areas where there is little choice of employment. The jobs involved in

Glamis Castle is the childhood home of another queen, Queen Elizabeth, the Queen Mother. Glamis is one of the many castles and stately homes open to the public. Some people like to follow a Castle Trail and visit several in one area.

tourism allow people to stay in their own part of the country instead of moving away to work.

At one time, visitors could rent a house or cottage for two to four weeks and stay in that area, but now the most popular vacation, particularly for those from outside Scotland, is to tour by car, bus, or train. Edinburgh, with its famous castle perched high on the Castle Rock above Princes Street, has always been popular with visitors, and Glasgow is getting more tourist traffic, particularly after the great success of its Garden Festival in the summer of 1988. Many people head north to the Highlands, although others find the time to stay a few days in the Borders of Scotland on their way north, something the Borders Tourist Board is trying to encourage.

For those who like a more active vacation, Scotland is popular for hill-walking and climbing, and in winter, skiing. The biggest skiing area is in the Cairngorm Mountains area above the Spey Valley. Scotland is also famous for golf and fishing, horseback and trail-riding.

Companies from abroad

Since the North British Rubber Company backed by American money moved into Edinburgh, and the American Singer Sewing Machine Company settled on Clydeside in the second half of the nineteenth century, Scotland has been attracting other companies from different countries. The Scottish agency, "Locate in Scotland," started 88 projects for new industry in 1988 and, if they are all successful, they could eventually provide up

Skiing is now a major source of income in the Highlands. The Aviemore Center, less than ten miles from the Cairngorm Mountains, now has a similar standard of hotels, chalets, and entertainment to that found in the big ski centers in Europe.

to 7,000 extra jobs in different areas. The majority of these overseas companies have headquarters in the United States.

As business and industry grows more international, some Scottish industrialists are hopeful that Scotland could benefit greatly after 1992 when the European Community becomes a single market. This means the countries of the European Community will then trade among themselves as though they were all one country, and there will be no import and export duties to pay. Many hope that this will bring strong direct links between Scotland and the Continent, instead of contact through London, and will revive the country's ties with Europe.

The oil industry
The effects of the oil industry in Scotland over the last 20 years have reached almost every corner of the country. Most affected is the whole northeast

---

Oil Facts

Commercial oil fields: 39, with 11 under development
Total employment: approximately 65,000
Employed in Grampian Region: 45,000
Biggest oil fields with estimated reserves:
Forties — 350 million tons
Brent — 265 million tons
Ninian — 155 million tons
Piper — 140 million tons
Total reserves 780-2.25 billion tons
Natural gas from U.K. Continental Shelf: 22,390 — 71,194 billion cubic feet
Oil fields for future development: 60

corner of the mainland, including the Moray and Cromarty Firths, and the Shetland and Orkney Islands off the north coast of the mainland. Aberdeen is called the "Oil Capital of Europe" and now has an international community and even an American school.

The history of oil is short and, when exploration started in the sixties, many Scots did not believe that enough oil would be found to form a large industry. Since then, the explosion in population and prosperity in the northeast has shown how wrong they were.

After the first major discovery in 1969, events moved quickly. New roads had to be built for increased traffic, as well as facilities to treat, store, and process the oil and gas.

Nowadays, oil goes by pipeline to three Scottish tanker terminals in Shetland, Orkney, and the Moray Firth, and natural gas comes ashore at St. Fergus in the Grampian Region. Around 65,000 people in Scotland are now employed in the oil industry or in industries that depend upon it, most of them either offshore, on the east coast, or in the northern islands.

Apart from bringing expansion and increased wealth to the northeast, the oil industry has had a much wider effect on Scotland. Large numbers of jobs have been created, both indirectly and as a result of the new industry. As well as the improved road and railway links, airports, too, have received needed improvements. In 1971, Aberdeen airport, for example, handled 140,000 passengers, but in 1986–1987, it handled 1.43 million passengers. Before the discovery of oil, Sumburgh airport in Shetland lay between golf

The Brent oil field off the coast of Scotland is large enough to support several oil rigs.

courses. Local golfers stopped playing when an aircraft was due. The new airport handled nearly half a million passengers in 1987.

Seaports have also seen changes since the coming of the oil industry. In the early 1970s, Aberdeen harbor, already the biggest in the area, expanded to cater to the oil industry and between 3,500 and 4,000 vessels now use it each year.

Scotland is now a center of research and education in oil and related technologies, with many research projects and training courses in Scottish universities and colleges, including the Institute of Offshore Medicine at Aberdeen University, and a School of Deep-sea Diving in Montrose. Because of the influx of people to the area, Aberdeen and the Grampian Region are among the most expensive places to live and buy a house in Scotland; however, Grampian has fewer people (7.84 percent) without work than any other part of Scotland.

Life on the drilling rigs and production platforms is hard. North Sea winds can gust to over 100 mph, and the seas are stormy. There is also an element of danger in working on the platforms, as was seen in July 1988 when the North Sea had its worst oil disaster. There was an explosion on the Piper Alpha platform, owned by the American company Occidental, that led to a terrible fire in which 167 people lost their lives.

Oil men usually go to the platform for perhaps two weeks and normally work a 12-hour shift. Many of those working offshore do not actually work to find or drill oil. They provide backup services such as preparing food, and each rig has its team of medical officers. Most companies provide movies and other entertainment for their employees working on the platforms. The standard of food is often so high that many oil workers find that they put on weight. Now oil companies have installed fitness and exercise rooms.

7 The Central Cities

The three major cities of the Central Lowlands, Edinburgh, Glasgow, and Dundee, although different in character, do have similarities.

All three are old cities, with ports and links with the sea, and each is a focal point for its own area and provides a wide variety of entertainment. There are theaters, restaurants, cinemas, sports fields, swimming pools, and ice rinks. City teenagers are more likely to go to a disco than to Scottish country dancing, although there are many popular clubs and societies where people take part in the traditional dances, and most pupils learn them at school. Not many Scots wear the traditional man's dress, the kilt, for daily wear. Many never wear a kilt at all, and others only wear it for evening occasions and at weddings and other celebrations.

Edinburgh has the largest dry-ski slope in Europe on the Penland Hills at its southern boundary, and all three cities have many golf courses. The Clyde estuary is one of the best sailing waters in Britain, and there is also sailing out of Edinburgh and Dundee.

Each city has its own soccer teams and, before and after every game, the streets near the fields are crowded with fans wearing their distinctive scarves and colors.

The arts in Scotland

Many of the national galleries and museums of Scotland are in Edinburgh, while Glasgow is the headquarters for most of the national performing

Edinburgh's skyline of church spires, towers, and hills provides a dramatic setting for a castle on its rocky outcrop. The city has resisted all attempts to allow high-rise developments to spoil the view.

companies. There are theaters, concert halls, galleries, museums, and performing companies all over Scotland.

The Scottish National Orchestra plays weekly during the winter in Edinburgh and Glasgow, and also holds regular concerts in Aberdeen and Dundee. Numerous small music groups perform all over Scotland, as do folk and pop groups, and both Edinburgh and Glasgow hold folk and jazz festivals. The Scottish Opera and Scottish Ballet, which has an associated school that combines dance with academic schoolwork, both operate from Glasgow.

The media

There are two national daily newspapers. *The Scotsman* is based in Edinburgh and the *Glasgow Herald* is based in Glasgow. *Scotland on Sunday* opened in August 1988 as the only Scottish Sunday paper. In addition there are two regional dailies, the *Aberdeen Press and Journal* and the *Dundee Courier,* and smaller local papers are published all over Scotland.

BBC Scotland is a national region of BBC (British Broadcasting Company) television. It makes its own programs and carries BBC United Kingdom network programs from London. It is financed by a government-controlled license fee. Scottish Independent Television companies are paid for by advertising between programs. These are Scottish Television, which covers Central Scotland, Grampian TV, covering the north of Scotland, and Border TV, which broadcasts to the border region between England and Scotland and to the Borders and Galloway. Television cable networks cover parts of Aberdeen and Glasgow.

BBC Radio Scotland covers all areas of Scotland and there are six commercial radio stations in Scotland based in Edinburgh, Glasgow, Aberdeen, Inverness, Dundee, and Ayr.

Edinburgh

Edinburgh's most famous street, Princes Street, has buildings on one side only. On the other side is the Castle Rock, on top of which stands Edinburgh Castle. The Castle is familiar to people all over the world because of television broadcasts of the Edinburgh Military Tattoo, which takes place on the Castle Esplanade.

Edinburgh Festival is not all classical music and serious theater. The city overflows with a collection of street musicians and entertainers of every sort.

The Royal Mile, which leads down to the Palace of Holyrood House, is the center of the Old Town, where once the city's people, from lord and merchant to servant, crowded together into large rat-infested buildings, divided into apartments known as tenements, or "lands." In the eighteenth century, an architect, James Craig, designed the New Town. Although today it is more than 200 years old it is still known by the same name. The New Town is north of the Castle and has kept its spectacular pattern of wide avenues and Georgian terraces, with two massive squares at each end of its central street.

Today, although it is a capital without a parliament, Edinburgh is still Scotland's administrative center and is the second-largest financial center in Great Britain after the City of London. It is also home to the Scottish Office, the Church of Scotland, and the highest courts, the Court of Sessions and the High Court of Justiciary.

Edinburgh has about two million visitors to the city each year. A good proportion of them like to visit at the time of the Edinburgh International Festival of Music and Drama held in August, the Edinburgh Military Tattoo, and the Festival Fringe, which attracts many professional and amateur companies.

Glasgow

Glasgow is Scotland's largest city, surrounded by some of the most beautiful countryside in Europe. The city's ornate public buildings were built when Glasgow was the second city of Victorian Britain, on riches from the engineering, shipbuilding, iron, steel and textile industries.

The Clyde River flows through the center of Glasgow. At one time, the great river was lined with shipyards, wharves, and ships from all over the world. Going "doon the water" (down the water) to one of the seaside towns along the Clyde was a typical Glaswegian pastime. The decline of Scotland's heavy industries left much of this part of the Clyde derelict and Glasgow had some of the worst slum areas in Britain.

The 1980s saw change and improvement to Glasgow, and in 1988 the south bank of the Clyde was resplendent with flowers and shrubs for the Glasgow Garden Festival, which was Britain's main event of that year, a mixture of gardening lore and entertainment. As Edinburgh has its

Much of Glasgow is being restored and Central Glasgow is once again, as it was in the nineteenth century, one of the best Victorian cities in Europe.

The 1988 Glasgow Garden Festival was the biggest public event in Glasgow since the city held the Great Empire Exhibition 50 years ago.

Festival of Music and Drama, Glasgow now has Mayfest, a festival of arts from circus to theater and rock music.

In 1990, Glasgow was the European City of Culture, taking over the title from cities that include Athens, Florence, and Paris. The city held an enormous program of cultural events and visiting orchestras and exhibitions of all kinds.

Dundee

Dundee is a city on a hill overlooking the Tay Estuary. Right into the present century, the port of Dundee had regular sea connections with places as far away as Russia, and its harbor was full of ships that brought in jute from India for the textile mills. It also had a flourishing shipbuilding industry and sent its own fleet of whalers to the Arctic each year.

In more recent years, Dundee has fared worse than any other Scottish city from the 1960s trend of demolishing old buildings and putting up new ones. Only one tower remains of the city's fortified wall, and much fine architecture has gone, after city planners destroyed good buildings along with the slums. In the nineteenth century, Dundee was an important center for the textile, jute, and shipbuilding industries, but the city has suffered decline in the twentieth century. It is only now beginning to show signs of regaining strength Dundee had the first continuous electricity supply in Scotland, and the revival of industry is largely due to the area's electronics and computer technology businesses. Today, Dundee produces more home computers than anywhere else in the country. Although the city is still suffering from unemployment, industries coming in are helping Dundee to become a prosperous city once more.

Dundee is near the mouth of the Tay River. In 1880 there was a terrible disaster when the long bridge that carried the railroad across the river collapsed. A passenger train and its carriages plunged into the river and sank.

8   Land, Loch, and Sea

The Highlands and Southern Uplands are the least populated areas of Scotland but many of the people who do live there depend on the land, the lochs, and the sea to make their living. It is also the home of many wild creatures.

Farming — Scotland's oldest industry

Farming has always been an important part of life in Scotland. Methods of farming have changed, but just over three-quarters of all Scottish land is still used for some form of farming. The farms in the upland areas tend to be big because the land is often difficult to cultivate and the climate is hard. Some mountain areas are so barren that they can support only a few animals on rough grazing.

Scotland has around eight million sheep, many of which live on the hills and are rounded up only twice a year for shearing, sorting, or for market.

The Blackface sheep is the best known of the Scottish hill sheep, seen everywhere and recognized by its black face and undocked tail. Its fleece is coarse and suitable for carpets and mattresses.

This large farm near Moffat is able to support arable farming and cattle on the lush grass of the valley bottom, while higher up the valley only sheep can make use of the poor pasture.

The farming industry employs nearly 50,000 people. The value of farming's total output is around $2.2 billion a year (1986). The type of farm depends on where it is. The wetter areas to the west that grow lush grass, and also many farms near big cities, specialize in dairying. Arable farms, which grow mostly crops, lie mainly in the fertile areas along the east coast, such as East Lothian, Tayside, or the Grampian Regions around Aberdeen.

The hilly areas of the country can only be used for breeding sheep and cattle, which are often fed on hay or straw bought from lowland farms.

Many lowland farmers fatten hill sheep and cattle on the rich lower pastures before the animals go to the butchers or meat traders.

Forestry

Forestry is also important in rural Scotland, and the country is home to half of the commercial forests (where trees are grown for timber) in Britain. Forests are planted on land unsuitable for farming, usually by the Forestry Commission, the public organization that owns most commercial forests. The Commission was set up in 1919, when woodlands had shrunk from the 60 percent of ancient times to only three percent of Scotland's land surface. The forestry industry also helps to provide work in rural areas.

Around 9,000 people work in the Scottish forests felling, logging, and planting, and another 2,500 work in wood processing.

Between 1919 and 1939, the Forestry Commission planted trees over 22,000 acres of Scotland in places as far apart as the Pentland Firth and the Mull of Kintyre. The planting still continues in the sparse upland. Each small tree is planted by hand.

When the Forestry Commission first started, trees were planted in dull, dark green rows that did not fit into the landscape. These ugly plantings are now disappearing as they become ready for felling, and modern foresters are paying more attention to the look of the land. Much of this change of style is due to Dame Sylvia Crowe, a landscape architect appointed by the Forestry Commission. She suggested making forestry more attractive by planting hardwood trees and larch to soften the outlines of conifer blocks, and leaving spaces along rivers and burns. In the last 20 years, the forests have almost doubled in size.

Many Scots like to spend their leisure time in the forests, walking and picnicking, and in 1935, the Forestry Commission opened the first forest park, the Argyll Forest Park, at the head of Loch Long, which is only 40 miles from Glasgow. Today, many forests, including private woods, are open to the public.

Fishing
Fishing is as old an industry as farming in Scotland. At one time the fishing communities were large and the boats small, but modern fishing is very different. Smaller numbers of fishermen now catch more fish and earn more money than their grandfathers and great-grandfathers. Modern fishing boats use all the latest nets, and radar and sonar equipment to track down and catch shoals of fish. Boats today can cost hundred of thousands of dollars.

Around 8,000 fishermen work in the industry. Some (mostly in the Western Isles, Shetlands, and Orkneys) work only part time. Many more people work in the business of fish processing and selling, or in building and repairing the fishing boats. Others make the ice to keep fish fresh, or produce the materials for boat building, engines, and other fishing equipment.

A lot of Scottish white fish is sold fresh, but some is processed, either by quick-freezing,

Aberdeen used to be Scotland's largest fishing port. Now Peterhead, farther north, has overtaken it as the largest fishing port in Europe.

Important Fishing Ports

East coast
Peterhead
Aberdeen
Fraserburgh
Macduff and Buckie (Moray Firth)
Lerwick (*Shetland Islands*)

West coast
Kinlochbervie
Mallaig
Ayr
Ullapool
Many smaller east and west coast ports also have fishing boats and shellfishermen.

curing, or smoking. Herring and mackerel are sold and exported fresh, quick-frozen, or are cured by various methods. Scottish shellfish are a delicacy and many are exported live to markets all over Europe. Five Scottish firms make fish meal and oil from fish such as sandeels, but these are not sold for human consumption.

Fish farming

The square and circular fish cages are a strange new sight in many western sea lochs and around the western and northern islands. A new breed of fish farm now rears thousands of fish until they are big enough for market. In salt water, the usual crop is salmon, but inland fish farms more often produce trout. Scotland now has over 1,600 fish farms.

Land, water, and conservation

The land and water are not only needed for farming, sport fishing, leisure, and tourism in Scotland, they are also home to natural wildlife, and Scotland is lucky to have some species that are either rare in other parts of Britain or not found at all. Such species include otter, wild cat, pine marten, and birds such as the sea eagle.

Despite its many open areas, like other countries, Scotland's natural environment faces dangers that include acid rain, the effects of farm or industrial chemicals on rivers and waterways, oil spills, and in some Highland areas, the planting of too many conifers.

The main method of looking after special nature areas is by forming nature reserves. In Scotland, the Nature Conservancy Council

Ospreys are fish-eating hawks that feed mostly on pike and trout. There are only a few pairs in Scotland and they are a protected species.

names Sites of Special Scientific Interest (SSSIs) that are of great importance to wildlife and the environment, and need special protection. Many other nature reserves are owned and managed by voluntary organizations, as places where people can watch wildlife without disturbing it. Conservationists also try to take care of the places surrounding the reserves by helping planners and developers to consider conservation needs in their plans.

Scottish Nature Facts

Biggest nature reserve: 97 square miles Cairngorms National Nature Reserve. Native Scots pine, alpine plants, many animals including reindeer, red deer, ptarmigan, crested tit.

Biggest Highland bird: Golden eagle, still found over many parts of the Highlands.

Smallest bird: goldcrest. Widespread in conifer plantations.

Biggest native land mammal: Red deer, 280 pounds. Widespread in Highlands, often graze on roadsides in severe, cold, winter weather.

Tallest tree: "Grand Fir," around 190 feet at Strone Gardens, east of Inveraray.

Oldest tree: Yew in Fortingall churchyard, north of Loch Tay. Probably over 3,000 years old.

Highest hedge: Meikleour, near Perth, has a beech hedge planted in 1746, now 85 feet high.

---

9 The Borders and Galloway

The Borders, and Dumfries and Galloway form the two local authority Regions that cover the Southern Uplands, although both Berwickshire in the east and Wigtownshire in the west also have fertile low-lying land. The Borders, which stretch almost to Edinburgh in the north, have a population of just over 100,000 while Dumfries and Galloway are home to nearly 150,000. Next to the Highlands and Islands, these two areas have the lowest population density in Scotland.

The regions are crossed by the Southern Upland Way, a long-distance footpath that runs for 210 miles between Portpatrick on the west coast and Cockburnspath in the east. In many places its route lies along the line of Scotland's old natural highways. These roads were mainly used by drovers, people whose job it was to drive the cattle to market.

A turbulent past

The Borders and Dumfriesshire form the border between England and Scotland. The border area was regularly fought over until 1603, when King James VI of Scotland became James I of both Scotland and England. The far west of Galloway was uninvolved in the border wars. Its links were strong with Ireland and even today the local accent is called "Galloway Irish." Many place names are Gaelic in origin, for example Kirk Madrine, meaning church of the little dogs.

Until the seventeenth century, the border between Scotland and England was frequently a battle area. Abbeys in the region, built by the monks in the eleventh and twelfth centuries, were raided and plundered on many occasions. Despite many attacks, Jedburgh Abbey is one of the best-preserved abbeys and was once the center of culture in the Borders.

Galloway was the headquarters of the Presbyterian group, the Covenanters, who had signed the National Covenant in 1638 to affirm their faith, and objected to the efforts of Charles I and Charles II to impose the English Episcopalian form of worship.

To avoid persecution, the Covenanters held outdoor services, and there are many memorials in Galloway at places where congregations were attacked and sometimes killed by troops.

From the small port of Portpatrick on the west coast, many Covenanters sailed to safety in Ireland. Others, less fortunate, sailed for America from Leith, the port of Edinburgh, as slaves. Persecution continued until Presbyterianism was restored in 1688.

Since 1984, archaeologists have been excavating ground at Whithorn to trace the history of the earliest known religious site in Scotland. This is the site of the fifth-century Latinus Stone, said to be the earliest Christian memorial in Scotland.

Border Names

Although the Borders were never Highland Clan country, the names of many old Border families are still very much in use today. Many telephone books will show lists of:

Elliots, Turnbulls, Douglases, Armstrongs, Rutherfords, Scotts, Grahams, Nixons, and more.

An Armstrong, the American astronaut Neil Armstrong, was the first man to set foot on the moon.

The Borders today

Green hills, upland farms, fields on either side of the roads, and small towns typify the rural setting of the Borders. Yet a higher proportion of people in the Borders work in industry than in many of the major Scottish industrial regions. This is a result of the development of a flourishing electronics industry. The towns are still small, the biggest being Hawick with a population of 16,000, but they are mostly industrial.

The traditional industry in the area uses wool. The Border tweed industry is centered on Galashiels and top-quality knitwear in Hawick, and many of the mills employ hundreds of people. Up until 20 years ago, most mills were family owned and operated. Today, although tweed and knitwear are still important to the Borders, many mills have become part of larger groups and some have closed.

All the Border towns celebrate an annual "Common Riding," a legacy of the days when the townspeople had to ride their marches (boundaries) to make sure no one had taken over any land or destroyed the markers. Selkirk's is the most famous of these "rides."

Dumfries and Galloway today

In the west, the mild climate produces lush, green grass and a longer growing season than other parts of Scotland. This makes Dumfries and Galloway rich farming and, particularly, dairy country. Big dairying companies such as the Scottish Milk Marketing Board, Unigate, and Express Dairies all have large, modern creameries in the region, and the milk tanker is a familiar sight on the narrow farm roads. The creameries make a local cheese, Galloway cheddar, and one creamery has branched out into its own version of Greek feta cheese.

Trees, forestry, and summer visitors

Forestry is important in Dumfries and Galloway because it is the most densely forested area in Scotland and one of the main centers of Britain's forestry industry. The biggest, the Galloway Forest Park, stretches north into Ayrshire and the Queen's Way passes through it between Newton Stewart and Dalry. This was planned by the Forestry Commission to show visitors places of special interest, such as the Galloway Deer Museum at Clatteringshaws Loch and, not far away, the Bruce's Stone, where King Robert the Bruce defeated the English by rolling large boulders down on top of them from above Loch Trool.

These huge forests provide millions of trees for sawmills, and, over the next 20 years, the Region expects that the number of sawmills will increase. Many sawmills have already expanded, and the Region has plans for other forms of wood manufacturing.

The trees and the long, dramatic coastline make tourism important to this area, and Galloway's main town, Stranraer on Loch Ryan, is the nearest Scottish port to Northern Ireland. Three miles farther east along the loch is Cairnryan, another small port. Leaving Loch Ryan, the North Channel that divides Scotland and Ireland narrows to around 20 miles. This has encouraged the route from Dumfries and Stranraer to become part of a Euro-route (a major highway) between Ireland and the Continent.

The main center

The biggest town in the whole area is Dumfries, where the Regional Council has its headquarters. It also has large industries such as the big polyester-film plant owned by Imperial Chemical Industries (ICI). However, in the past few years, many smaller industries and craft workshops have grown up all over Dumfries and Galloway, from knitwear in the east to salmon farming and salmon smoking on the west coast.

10 The Highlands and Western Isles

The Highlands and Islands takes in the whole of the northwest of Scotland and the Western Isles and covers an area bigger than either Wales or Belgium. Yet only around 250,000 people live in this huge, empty land, just over 0.5 percent of the total population of the United Kingdom.

Here, the mountains are higher, the distances greater between villages and towns, and the roads wind more than anywhere else in Scotland. The region's history and culture are different from the rest of Scotland and this is the stronghold of the Gaelic language.

In days gone by, to Lowlanders the Highlands and Western Isles were mysterious and unknown. They were ruled, until 1493, from the Isle of Skye by chiefs of Clan Donald, who bore the title the Lord of the Isles.

Although there was fighting among the clans, it was not a primitive society. Gaelic culture, tradition, and law flourished and the "learned classes" who knew medicine, poetry, history, music, law and many crafts were honored.

In 1746, after the battle of Culloden, many clan chiefs were exiled and their lands taken. The ban on the bagpipes, tartan, and the right to carry weapons, imposed by the government in London after the battle, damaged the Highlanders' pride and sense of identity, and the long years of emigration put a final end to the clan system.

The Highlands and Islands did not have an

SS Metegma ran aground in the St. Lawrence Seaway as she carried immigrants from Scotland to a new life in Canada. In the 1920s, with every voyage from Scotland, some islanders left for the New World.

Industrial Revolution, but Highland families left in the hundreds to work in the shipyards and mills of Glasgow and the south. Emigration continued into the twentieth century and the greatest numbers left between 1911 and 1931, when the population fell by 50,000.

The last great tide of emigration forced various governments to realize that something had to be done, and they created plans to breathe new economic life into these beautiful, remote areas. The Forestry Commission was the first important influence. Later on help came for the fishing industry from the Herring Industry Board.

Traditional work

Only 10 percent of the work force today earn their living in farming, fishing, and forestry, but this traditional work is still important to the Highland way of life and the use of land and sea.

There are deer and grouse on the mountains and moorland, and there are some very large sporting estates where field sports such as hunting and shooting are the best in the world. Some estates now farm deer.

The Uplands have hill sheep farms and, less high up, cultivated ground can be sown with grass or sometimes planted with cereal crops.

In some areas, particularly in Caithness, sheep and deer are being replaced by trees. Forestry provides income in many parts of the Highlands.

One special form of farming is carried out in this region, particularly on the west coast and on the islands, that is called crofting. A croft is usually only a few acres of arable land around the farmer's house and is set in a group of crofts, called a township. Much of the grazing land around the township is shared.

Many crofters are only farmers in their spare time because a croft is rarely large enough to support a family. A crofter might also work as a coastguard or forester, and on the islands will perhaps have a boat for fishing or even a few fish-farming cages.

Crofters often share jobs and equipment. They will combine to gather the sheep for clipping, take turns with a tractor, and throughout the summer, both men and women work together to cut the community's winter fuel of peat, which they cut from the moorland peat banks.

This dam high up at the northern end of Loch Awe helps provide a head of water for the Cruachan hydroelectric power station. At the base, visitors can go a mile inside the "hollow mountain" to see the hydroelectric power station excavated out of the rock, invisible from outside.

Industry

A really dramatic change in the fortunes of the Highlands began when, around 1943, the North of Scotland Hydroelectric Board began to generate electricity by building dams and power stations. This meant that new industries were possible, such as aluminum smelting, and pulp and paper milling.

Large-scale manufacturing and heavy industry are to be found in the east part of the Highlands and Islands. The Dounreay Nuclear Power

Development Establishment that opened in the 1950s, together with improved road and rail links, helped to attract industry to the area.

Also in the east, the towering metal rigs and platforms are proof of the work that North Sea oil has brought to the Moray and Cromarty Firths. The oil terminal at Nigg in the Cromarty Firth also receives oil pumped through underwater pipes from the North Sea.

Alongside the heavy industry and the North Sea oil industry of the Highlands, there are smaller industries ranging from electronics to seaweed gathering and processing. Many tiny communities have a craft workshop that sells their various wares either direct to tourists or through a local craft shop.

Ullapool on the northwest coast provides a pleasant harbor for fishing and sailing boats. It is also a center for small industries and tourism in the northwest Highlands in Loch Broom.

Tourism

When people say Scotland, they usually think of the Highlands, and that vision brought over two million visitors north in 1988 to spend over $425 million. In the small communities, where people provide bed and breakfast in their own homes, or run hotels and many other enterprises set up to bring in the tourists, money from visitors is an important part of their livelihood.

Highland towns

In the Highlands and Islands, even small towns are towns rather than overgrown villages, with a life different from that of the countryside around them. Towns around the Moray Firth such as Invergordon, Dingwall, Nairn, and Forres vary in population from around 2,000 to 6,000 people. The main Spey Valley towns in the tourist, and skiing areas are Grantown-on-Spey and Aviemore. Farther west are Fort William, Ullapool, and Oban, which is the main tourist center of that part of the Highlands. Off Oban are some of the finest sailing waters in western Europe. The most northerly Scottish mainland town is Thurso, just a few miles across the Pentland Firth from the Orkney Islands.

Inverness, with a population of 40,000, is called the "capital" of the Highlands. It is the biggest town in the north and a center for work, business, shopping, and entertainment. It is the home of Highland Regional Council and the Eden Court Theatre. This is the biggest theater in the Highlands and provides theater, music, and dance.

The Ness River flows through the city on its short journey from Loch Ness to the Moray Firth,

The Loch Ness Monster

A popular tourist spot is Loch Ness where people come all year round in the hope of spotting the famous Loch Ness Monster. Many people claim to have seen this strange, serpentlike water creature, and in 1934 a man called Robert Wilson took a photograph of a dark shape looming out of the water that many believe was the monster. Still no one knows for sure and the search has become scientific rather than treasure hunting. The Lochside Centre, opened in 1980, has a model to show the visitors what they should be looking for when monster-spotting.

and the city looks out to the Black Isle and distant mountains. The battlefield of Culloden Moor with its great grave mounds is only three miles away.

The Western Isles

The Western Isles stretch from the giant cliffs of the Butt of Lewis in the north for 200 miles to the south of Islay. Around 80 islands are inhabited, some with only a lighthouse and a handful of people. Most are rocky islets uninhabited by humans.

The Outer Hebrides

Far to the northwest is the long narrow spine of the Outer Hebrides. From north to south, the main islands are Lewis and Harris, which form one island, North Uist, Barra, South Uist, Benbecula, the little island of Eriskay, and Vatersay.

Almost every croft has its "loom shed." To make genuine Harris Tweed, the crofter must use only human power to drive the loom.

The largest town of these islands is Stornoway on Lewis, which has a population of 6,000 and is the home of the Western Island Council, covering Lewis and Harris. Life in Stornoway is much the same as small town life anywhere in Scotland acting as a center for schools and entertainment for the crofting townships outside.

In Lewis and Harris, weaving Harris tweed is an important part of the income of a crofter, whose home-woven cloth is labeled with the "Orb" trademark of genuine Harris Tweed.

The Inner Hebrides

Farther south, the chain of islands begins to spread out. Through its links with Bonnie Prince Charlie and *The Skye Boat Song*, Skye is probably the best-known Scottish island. It is as far north as the Uists but nearer to the mainland, and its volcanic origins give it a dramatic mountain landscape in the Cuillins. This is shared by the two smaller islands to the south, Rhum and Eigg, and also Mull, which is only an hour by ferry from Oban on the mainland. Mull and the smaller islands of Tiree, Coll, and the Holy Isle of Iona,

The island of Islay has eight distilleries and some of its best malt whiskies owe their flavor to the peat smoke used to malt, or germinate and dry, the barley.

Loganair aircraft on Barra's beach landing strip. This is an airport where the timetables depend on the tide!

the center of St. Columba's Celtic Church, look to Oban as their mainland link.

Even farther south are the little island of Colonsay and the mountainous peaks of Jura (Deer Island) which is largely sporting estates. Last of all comes Islay, with its long, golden beaches, dramatic cliffs, and a golf course of championship standard.

Getting around

Transportation is very important, bringing together isolated crofting townships, and linking the islands. Loganair provides a network of local air services, and car and passenger ferries connect the islands to Kyle of Lochalsh, Mallaig, and Oban which all have railroad stations. A proposal made in 1989 for a bridge link to Skye, which is only five minutes by ferry from Kyle, will probably take many years to build.

Despite the distances, the Outer Hebrides earned around $27 million from tourism in 1988 and the more accessible Inner Hebrides are always popular with visitors. Although tourism means new prosperity, many islanders are eager to ensure that the slower pace of life is not lost.

Getting around the islands can be slow. The Highland roads bend and twist but many roads have now been much improved and, by using a careful mixture of bus and ferry, and timing it well, you can travel around most of the islands on public transportation.

11

The Northern Islands — Orkney and Shetland

Orcadians, the people of Orkney, and Shetlanders scarcely think of themselves as Scots. They talk about "going to Scotland" as they board the plane or boat for Aberdeen, and the biggest island in each group is called Mainland.

There are scarcely any trees on these northerly islands. In the face of the constant wind that sweeps in from the sea, vegetation seldom grows taller than three feet. The weather is always warmer in winter than might be expected so far north, despite the wind, but it can also be very changeable with sun, rain, wind, and even sleet all in one day. The mildness is due to the influence of the Gulf Stream, the changeability from the nearness of the sea all around.

A Viking past

Nowhere has the Viking influence on Scotland proved stronger than in Shetland and Orkney. This is not surprising since the islands were part of Norway from around 800 to 1469. This Scandinavian influence lasted for 650 years, longer than the islands have been part of modern Scotland.

Language

Orkney and Shetland place names are almost all of Norse origin. Until around 200 years ago, Shet-

This Viking ship off Lerwick is a reconstruction of a Viking longship. It is named Odin's Raven *and is rowed by Shetlanders, in celebration of their Viking heritage.*

land had its own language, called Norn, and there are still around 10,000 words of Scandinavian origin used today and an old Norn dictionary. BBC Radio Shetland, a small outstation of BBC Scotland, produces regular programs in the dialect, and interest continues in the Norn language.

The January festival of Up-Helly-Aa is also Viking in origin and is based on the old pagan fire festivals. Processions of *guizers* in armor and winged helmets carry burning torches to set alight a replica of a Viking longship. This is not a festival put on for the tourist but part of island life.

Orkney
Orkney's low-lying, undulating land is fertile,

and many Orcadians are farmers. Its southernmost island, Ronaldsay, is only six miles from the Scottish mainland, and the highest point is Hoy which rises to 1,565 feet, and has Britain's highest vertical cliffs at 1,140 feet.

There are 67 islands, and just under 20,000 people live on 18 of them. By far the greatest proportion live on Mainland, with its two towns, Kirkwall with a population of 6,680, Orkney's capital, and Stromness where 2,160 live. Orkney can claim to have Scotland's most northerly whisky distillery, at Kirkwall, and whisky has been made here since 1798.

Orkney's most famous archaeological site is at Skara Brae, dating back 5,000 years. It is the best-preserved Stone Age village in Europe, dramatically uncovered in 1850 when its blanket of sand blew away in a storm. St. Magnus Cathedral, which celebrated its 850th anniversary in 1987, is the focal point for one of the most remote Music Festivals in the world, founded by the composer Peter Maxwell Davies who lives in Orkney.

Shetland

Shetland is Scotland's northernmost outpost, level with the tip of Greenland, and as far from London as London is from Genoa, in Italy.

Fifteen of Shetland's 100 islands are inhabited, and its biggest island is Mainland. It is 55 miles long and 20 miles across at its widest point, but its deeply indented coastline means that no point is more than a few miles from the sea.

Shetlanders have long traveled the world as sailors and fishermen. The main fishing harbor of

Shetland is famous for its knitting, which like weaving is a home industry. The special patterns all have different meanings.

Lerwick, Shetland's "capital" is full of Scandinavian, French, German, and Russian flags flying from the masts of ships in the harbor.

Crofting, sheep-farming, and fishing play important roles in the economy of the islands. Many islanders have a boat for fishing or leisure, and Shetland people have taken so strongly to the relatively new salmon-farming industry that it is soon expected to overtake fish landings in value.

Living with oil

Oil came to the northern islands when work started on the construction of British Petroleum's oil terminal at Sullum Voe, which brought 2,000 construction workers into Shetland. They lived in specially built new hostels, some of which have been turned into hotels and guest houses since the terminal opened in 1978. The new terminal has meant new schools, new health centers, and other public services.

Shortly after it opened, Shetland's Sullum Voe terminal had its first oil spill, which killed hundreds of birds and even sheep on the Shetland beaches. This led to joint action between the oil companies and local conservationists who have devised an elaborate system to prevent damage and monitor the effects of oil on wildlife and the ocean around Shetland. BP has invested in an emergency system, at a cost of $1.7 million, to clean up any oil spills or slicks.

Apart from the work and money it has brought into these distant islands, the benefit of oil to

The cliffs of the Shetland Isles provide an excellent nesting place for many sea birds, including puffins.

Shetland and Orkney is that it prevented an inevitable decline when Scotland's industry in general began to suffer.

Both Island Councils have used their oil money to invest in improving roads, hotels, houses, and other lasting benefits so that, when and if the oil runs out, it will leave behind many of the gains it has brought to the islands.

Island wildlife

Both Shetland and Orkney are famous for their birdlife and naturalists come from all over the world to visit the cliffs and island stacks, where seabirds nest in the thousands, and to watch seals and otters in their natural habitat. The island of Fetlar in Shetland is the only place in Britain where snowy owls have bred in modern times.

12 The Future

Scotland has retained a stubborn identity of its own, part of, but not the same as, the rest of Great Britain. Can this special character continue in a world of fast travel, computers that pass instant information, and satellites beaming pictures and sounds from all over the world?

In many ways the sense of Scottish identity is as strong today as it has always been. Scottish life and culture have remained vital and thriving by adapting themselves to change. This is particularly noticeable in the arts. In recent years, the theater, cinema, and other arts have flourished, often drawing upon older Scottish traditions but placing them in the context of today.

Although there are many people unemployed, most Scots have a good standard of living and the economy has improved. In recent years, the oil industry has suffered setbacks but these seem to have been largely overcome for the moment. However, Scotland still needs to provide jobs for the many people who are still out of work through no fault of their own.

For many years there has been talk of independence or devolution from England. The introduction by the government in Westminster of unpopular political measures, such as the Community Charge or Poll Tax, has strengthened the call for self-government. Can this be brought about in a way that retains ties with the rest of Britain? Is such hostility to government from Westminster another peak in a series of waves of

The Royal High School in Edinburgh no longer functions as a school. If Scotland ever achieves independence the building is considered a likely location for the new government.

nationalism? There remain doubts as to whether self-determination is more of a possibility for Scotland today than it has been in previous times.

Scotland has most of the wilderness areas of Britain, which grow increasingly important as pressure for space continues. While there have been many benefits to the Scottish economy from tourism, these areas are at risk from many different types of pollution, to the land, sea, and air. The growth of the nuclear power industry in these remote regions raises serious questions about the long-term safety effects and protection of the environment. Pollution of the seas around the Scottish coast is a matter for concern because it endangers the natural marine environment and in particular certain types of wildlife such as seals, which are common in Scottish waters. How can these wild and beautiful areas be protected from poorly planned development?

Though these questions are important, the most vital date facing Scotland is 1992—the start of a true "European common market," with free trade and no import and export controls between the countries of Europe. Will Scotland find itself pushed even farther away from the heart of Europe, or will the old Scottish-European links of the past spring to life again?

Index

Raeburn, Henry 32
Red Clydeside 23
Redpath, Ann 32
religion 18, 25, 29-30
    Catholic 30
    Covenanters 68
    Protestant 18, 29, 30
Rhinns Peninsula 13-14
rivers 10, 11, 12, 78-79
Romans 15

St. Columba 82
Scoti 15
Scott, Sir Walter 12, 13
Scottish National Party 24
Shetland Islands 48 84, 85, 86-89
Simpson, Sir James Young 31
Skara Brae 86
Skye, Island of 10, 73, 81
Smith, Adam 31
social services 30
Southern Uplands 8-9, 12-13, 67
Spey River 11

sports 33-34, 51
    Scots sports 34
Staffa 10
Stevenson, Robert Louis 32
Stornaway 80

Tay River 12, 15
tourism 44-46, 78, 83
transportation, 72, 77, 82-83
Tweed River 12

unemployment 39, 40, 41, 90
Union of the Crowns 17

Victoria, Queen 44

Western Isles 30, 79
wildlife 65-66, 89
Wilkie, David 32
William of Orange 19, 20
World War I 23-24
World War II 39

This edition originally published 1990 by Heinemann Children's Reference, a division of Heinemann Educational Books, Ltd.